Success:

A Way of Life

T.C.H The Author

Success: A Way of Life

Dedicated to everyone that has a goal and striving to be successful in life. Everyone has one thing in common when each of us wakes up, and that's the power to strive for greatness on the road to success to make a way of life.

SUCCESS

A WAY OF LIFE

T.C.H The Author
copyright (c) 2018 by T.C.H The Author
All rights reserved. Your vision LLC
Published (p) in the United States by
T.C.H The Author

ISBN 978-0-9985032-0-2
eBook ISBN 978-0-9985032-1-9

Without limited the rights under copyright reserved above, no part of this publication may be reproduced, stored in or introduced into a retrieval system, or transmitted, in any form, or by any means (electronic, mechanical, photocopying, recording, or otherwise), without the prior written permission of both the copyright owner and above publisher of this book

Success: A Way of Life

Acknowledgement

    I would like to take a moment to thank some of the people who have come into my life in order to aid in my visions, helping me to get to the next step of my ladder. Thank you to everybody who assisted me, my experiences life gave to me, as well as to those who inspired me to write this book. It takes a great team to help a vision come to pass. I am successful because I saw myself as so, and because I have a great team that saw my light. Appreciate you all!

I am

T.C.H, The Author

S

Start your journey with a vision.

U

Only **U** can guide yourself through your life's path.

C

Create a goal you wish to strive for.

C

Climb over any hurdles you may encounter.

E

Erase all negativity from your mind.

S

Stay positive throughout any storms.

S

Study and implement what you have learned.

Table of Contents

Introduction ……………………………….
16
Confidence ……………………………….
19
Trust ……………………………………….
21
Vision ………………………………………
24
Timing ……………………………………...
26

Preparation ……………………………….
28
Patience ………………………………….
30
Decisions ………………………………..
31
Focus ……………………………………..
32
Delayed Gratification ………………
33
Opportunity ……………………………
35
Perception ………………………………
37
Listening ………………………………..
39
Conclusion ……………………………..
46

Introduction

In this book, I have provided all of the keys that helped me strive to become the success I am today. Success is only limited by your desires and the power of the imagination. This is the act of envisioning yourself in certain positions, such as an entrepreneur, a business owner, or even a songwriter until your visions become reality. Your true success is the understanding that you are the master of your own destiny.

I grew up in a place called New Haven, Connecticut. I am not quite sure how or why, but growing up, I had a knack for obtaining what I wanted. Back then, I somehow knew, if I focused long enough, it would find its way to me. As I grew older, I would become a much more complexed thinker. I often would find myself pondering over thoughts of "Why do things happen a certain way?', and 'How did this person get to where they are now?'

I didn't quite get it until I received some rather wise advice. In life, in order to capture great moments, I must know how to move. What do I mean by *move*? In some ways, life, it can be compared to a simple ladder. Ladders have several steps, each one is slightly higher than the one before it. It is a similar concept in life, in order to succeed in life, one must position their moves appropriately to achieve the next step. For example, if a person wants to be in a certain position in their career, that person must behave as if they're already in that position. I took this advice to heart, and I have used it in my daily life ever since.

If you embrace the keys that this book provides, and utilize them in your own life, you too will reach your own version of success.

Confidence

Key number one is confidence. Having confidence is one of the most effective keys in your journey to creating success. Throughout your journey we all call life, you will interact with a countless number of people; all with different backgrounds, beliefs, and logic. It is essential to display confidence no matter the encounter.

This is especially true in corporate; it is necessary to exude confidence when building a brand, business, or company. How can anyone else believe, or buy into you, if you do not believe in yourself? It is not possible. If you want to grow professionally, you have to believe you are not only worthy of attaining your goal; but you will reach it no matter what. You must understand that you are there to win. Never allow anyone to break your spirit or cause you to lose your focus. You must stand tall, like the Eiffel Tower, indestructible by the turbulence that may be surrounding you. The confidence you possess will directly affect how successful you will become in your life, and how well you will embrace the success that you so rightfully deserve.

Trust

Key number two is trust. Trust is equally important as possessing confidence. It is the essence in life for self-reassurance. Trust is a tricky trait, as it can take as long as a lifetime to build, it can take as little as a second to destroy. It takes a lot of energy to create, and barely any to demolish. Develop a trust in knowing everything is going to work out in the best way possible.

Just as there is a level of trust when your job deposits a check into your bank account. You know your money is going to be there when you decide to withdraw it. You must trust your friends, and significant other to be supportive of your goals and dreams.

    Even more importantly, you must trust yourself. No matter the level of difficulty in life's obstacles, it should not alter your trust in yourself. The knowledge to do what is necessary is already instilled within your mind, trust your inner self. Unlock your hidden potential. Embrace it. Take Action. Think of it as your internal compass guiding your steps along the way to your goals. Have faith that everything will go according to the vision you see for yourself. By doing this, you will achieve the success you seek. Your journey to success will unfold as it should.

As it is said, everything happens for a reason. Have you have ever heard the quote; *It was Written in the Stars?* This is when the universe is in perfect alignment with the stars which constructs your path in life. It is also known as fate. Trust fate. It is the development of events beyond a person's control, regarded as determined by a supernatural power. Having the faith that no matter what choice you make you will be guided back to your destiny. Trust in that, and trust you will be successful.

Vision

Key number three is having a vision. Each goal is just something you've completed without a larger "why" in mind. Vision is your why. Having a Vision gives you direction. It is your desired future. Your purpose. Vision is not what we see with our eyes; but what we see with our minds. Everything in life is about having a mental picture of your goals. Focus on what it takes to reach each of those goals and execute them. Your vision is your passion as it keeps you excited and motivated. It's what inspires you to do whatever it is you want to do to achieve your goals.

Keep in mind, all things and everything in life is a process, it takes time to develop and expand your horizon. Have the patience, trust, and confidence in your vision to see it grow. So much can happen within a six month period. If only you are willing to go through the process. Therefore, if you don't have a vision, goals alone can be defeating.

Timing

Key number four is timing. Everything we do in life is about timing. This is a crucial part of the planning and achieving your goals. It is said that fate puts us in the right place at the right time in order to maximize our greatest opportunities. Once you've timed you next move correctly, it will seem as though everything that follows will fall into place.

For example, two boxers in the ring, the first boxer hastily throws a jab and doesn't land it. The other throws the same jab, but this fighter, he waits for the right opportunity by timing his jab. The second fighter's jab lands, he quickly follows up with a hook, and ultimately wins the match. Waiting for the right moment to strike is vital to your success.

A wise man once said, "for every negative find the positive within it." Think like that boxer in the ring. See life as the opponent, seize the right opportunities, and always be ready to strike at the right moment. Each and every one of us gets twenty-four hours to do what we desire. It is what to choose to do within our twenty-four hours that will determine the level of our success we obtain.

Preparation

Key number five is preparation. I believe preparation plus opportunity equals success.

It is the action or process of being made ready. You must be ready to become the process of achieving your goals. Envision your plan of execution. Plan your steps. Have faith, confidence, and the courage to take action. Nothing comes without preparation.

A boxer trains for a fight, an artist rehearses to give a great show, a speaker gathers up ideas to speak about a topic of discussion. All of that is preparation for greatness. There is a saying; *Repetition is the father of learning*. This is when a person repeats the same action in preparation for what is to come. Preparing the mind to conquer whatever is the most valuable skill.

Patience

Key number six is patience. Today, not many people practice patience; they want their results instantly. As the saying goes, *Rome was not built in a day.* Having patience is a rare trait, but it is a necessity for reaching your goals. for the more, you wait on something to happen the more you can Cherish it when it does happen.

As we go through life, we encounter obstacles which prevent us from reaching our goals. This is when we need to trust the process and not to be so quick to give up. Everything you strive to do you must have the patience to ensure the best in order to get the greatest results on your journey.

Decisions

Key number seven is decisions. When achieving goals, it is critical to make the best decisions. It is the action or resolution reached after consideration. In any situation, a person must consider the whole picture and make a rational decision.

Our decisions are like a road map for our success journey. We have the option to go left, straight, or right; our outcome is a direct result of our choices. Choose wisely. It will impact your journey towards success. Take the time to think about it, so that you can realistically assess the situation. Create a clear picture of the consequences for yourself. Decide what you want. Make a plan and work on that plan every single day.

Focus

Key number eight is focus. What is your center of interest? What is it that you desire to do the most? Having focus plays an important role in becoming successful. If you want to achieve the success your striving for, you must focus on goals, in business or personal affairs. To focus means to direct time and attention to a limited number of issues. Things that are outside your selected area of focus becomes unimportant. It's best not to focus on the distraction.

Although, I Understand that you may lose focus along the way. Acknowledge it and refocus yourself. Why did you start your journey to success? What steps are needed to reach your goal towards success?

Delayed Gratification

Key number nine is delayed gratification. It is the ability to resist the temptation for an immediate reward and waiting for a later reward. Generally, delayed gratification is associated with resisting a smaller but more immediate reward in order to receive a larger more enduring reward later.

For example, having the choice to receive one hundred dollars today or wait a week to receive twice the amount. Which would you choose? Start small, think small in order to get big. It is a process. Start from the bottom, create a solid foundation and build from there. In your journey to success, you will encounter many opportunities to learn and grow. Embrace the knowledge you receive to expand your horizon. Anyone who is open to learning can only become wiser and better. Trust yourself. Trust the process. Have the patience to get through it even if you temporarily lose focus. Regain your focus and have the confidence to make your vision a reality. Don't look for the instant result because as the saying goes, anything worth having is worth waiting for.

Opportunity

Key number ten is opportunity. It is defined as a set of circumstances that makes it possible to do something. Be it a chance for employment or promotion. Learning how to recognize a good opportunity is a great asset. It is a useful or valuable human quality to push farther in life. When an opportunity presents itself have the confidence in yourself to take it.

Although every opportunity presented is not meant to be accepted; each and every day we have the choice to either open the door or walk away. If you choose to walk away from an opportunity, have the patience to wait. Always believe there is a better opportunity for you in the future. One will be more beneficial to you and your vision. Choosing what is best for you will help you evolve and climb the ladder to success.

Perception

Key number eleven is perception. Having the ability to see, hear, or become aware of a situation is vital to choose what opportunities are right for you. Everything we see and hear aren't always what we believe them to be. We have to be about to decipher the difference. What is real and what is fake. What is good and what is bad.

For example, reality T.V., it is the director's perception that is being shown as something real. We now know that reality T.V. is, in fact, one hundred percent scripted, it's just an illusion. But we choose to be entertained even knowing it is not real. We know not to take it seriously.

The art of perception is being able to step back to observe a situation and make the perfect decision. If you can do this, you will be able to obtain your desired goals.

Listening

Key number twelve is listening. It is the key to all effective communication. Without the ability to listen effectively, messages are easily misunderstood. The inability to listen will only lead to not learning what you need in order to grow. This is a skill that most people lack.

You may have heard the saying, "We have two ears but only one mouth." This is an easy way to remember that listening can be twice as important as talking. As a student, you most likely spend many hours in a classroom doing large amounts of focused listening. Yet it's sometimes difficult to apply those efforts to communicate in other areas of your life. As a result, your listening skills may not be all they could be.

As you become aware of this flaw, you will be more mindful to improve. The more you listen, the more you learn. The more you learn, the more successful you will become once you apply what you've learned. Knowledge is power. Listen, retain it, and use it to fuel your journey towards success.

At the end of the day, invest in yourself. No goal can be achieved without hard work.

Think about your success

Write down your Goals

Write down why you want these goals to manifest

Enjoy your now while visualizing about your later

Enjoy your success

Conclusion

Throughout life, we all strive to reach our various goals. There's no accurate way to success. As we are all different so too are the paths we take to reach them. I have provided the twelve keys that will ensure your success.

WISH YOU WELL!

T.C.H The Author